SECRETS OF THE MUMMIES

D1707416

FIRST EDITION
Project Editors Mary Atkinson and Penny Smith; **Art Editor** Karen Lieberman;
Senior Editor Linda Esposito; **US Editor** Regina Kahney; **Pre-Production** Francesca Wardell;
Picture Researchers Andy Sampson and Kathy Lockley; **Illustrator** Peter Dennis;
Reading Consultant Linda Gambrell, PhD

THIS EDITION
Produced for DK by WonderLab Group LLC
Jennifer Emmett, Erica Green, Kate Hale, *Founders*
www.wonderlabgroup.com

Editors Grace Hill Smith, Libby Romero, Michaela Weglinski;
Photography Editors Kelley Miller, Annette Kiesow, Nicole DiMelle; **Managing Editor** Rachel Houghton;
Product Manager Sarah Forbes; **Design Director** Phil Ormerond; **Production** Andrew Beehag;
Designers Project Design Company; **Jacket Style Designer** Lisa Lanzarini; **Researcher** Michelle Harris;
Copy Editor Lori Merritt; **Indexer** Connie Binder; **Proofreader** Larry Shea; **Production** Andrew Beehag;
Reading Specialist Dr. Jennifer Albro; **Curriculum Specialist** Elaine Larson

Published in the United States by DK Publishing
1745 Broadway, 20th Floor, New York, NY 10019

Copyright © 2023 Dorling Kindersley Limited
DK, a Division of Penguin Random House LLC
22 23 24 25 26 10 9 8 7 6 5 4 3 2 1
001-333862-May/2023

All rights reserved.

Without limiting the rights under the copyright reserved above, no part of this publication may be reproduced, stored in or
introduced into a retrieval system, or transmitted, in any form, or by any means (electronic, mechanical, photocopying,
recording, or otherwise), without the prior written permission of the copyright owner.
Published in Great Britain by Dorling Kindersley Limited

A catalog record for this book
is available from the Library of Congress.
HC ISBN: 978-0-7440-7111-5
PB ISBN: 978-0-7440-7112-2

DK books are available at special discounts when purchased in bulk for sales promotions, premiums,
fundraising, or educational use. For details, contact: DK Publishing Special Markets,
1745 Broadway, 20th Floor, New York, NY 10019
SpecialSales@dk.com

Printed and bound in China

The publisher would like to thank the following for their kind permission to reproduce their images:
a=above; c=center; b=below; l=left; r=right; t=top; b/g=background

Alamy Stock Photo: dpa picture alliance / Sebastian Kahnert 45clb; **Dreamstime.com:** Andrey Donnikov 26tl, Sl Photography 29b;
Getty Images: AFP / Bruno Ferrandez 45tr, Hulton Archive 16tl, 21b, Hulton Fine Art Collection / Art Images 22tr

Cover images: *Front:* **Dreamstime.com:** Jaroslav Moravcik b; **Getty Images:** Mint Images; *Back:* **Shutterstock.com:** Little.Kalu cla,
Macrovector cra, cl

All other images © Dorling Kindersley
For more information see: www.dkimages.com

For the curious
www.dk.com

Level
4

SECRETS
OF THE
MUMMIES

Harriet Griffey

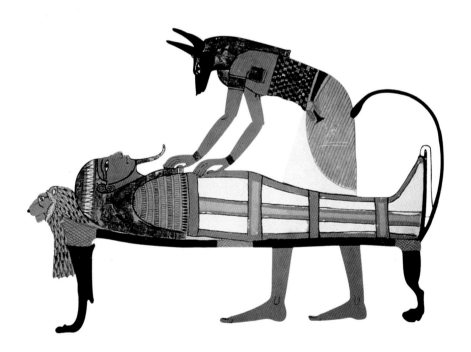

CONTENTS

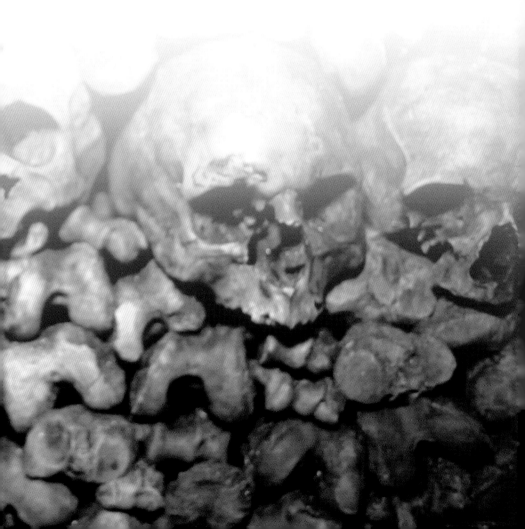

Teenage Boy
Some Roman mummies were decorated with a realistic painting of the person who had died.

Animals
The ancient Egyptians believed cats were sacred. They often mummified cats' bodies when they died.

PEOPLE FROM THE PAST

There is something intriguing about a mummy. It is hard to believe that hundreds or even thousands of years ago it was a living person.

A mummy is the preserved body of someone who has died. The body may have been preserved naturally or deliberately as part of a religious ritual.

Naturally preserved bodies have been discovered in airless bogs. Here, the animals and bacteria that usually break down bodies cannot survive, so the body does not decay. This can also happen in hot, dry deserts and on icy mountains.

This mummy was found in a Danish bog. It is the body of a man who died more than 1,500 years ago.

Other bodies were carefully preserved by people. The most famous mummies belong to the ancient Egyptians. But other cultures, such as the Incas of South America and the Pazyryks of Siberia, also used to preserve their dead. Some people buried their mummies with artifacts, such as bowls, statues, and beautiful jewels.

This book investigates different mummies discovered around the world. We'll look first at how the ancient Egyptians made a mummy.

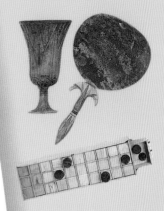

Artifacts
Everyday objects were often buried with mummies.

Important Doll
Figures, such as this Peruvian doll, were buried with a mummy to bring the dead person luck in the afterlife.

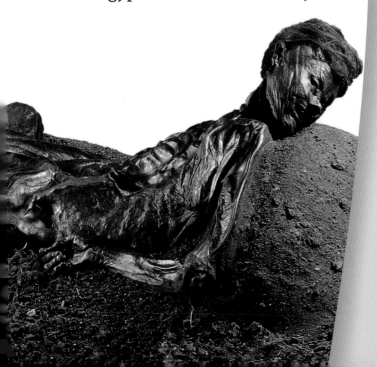

7

Temple Guardians
A chief priest represented the king and the gods. He looked after a temple and performed certain rituals.

Statue of an Egyptian priest

Embalming
Chemicals, perfumes, and balms are used in this process to stop a body from decaying.

MAKING A MUMMY

For 3,000 years, the ancient Egyptian civilization flourished. The people living then had strong beliefs about gods and life after death. They thought that if a dead person's spirit could recognize its preserved body, it would live forever in the afterlife.

Wealthy Egyptians paid the chief priests to mummify the bodies of their loved ones. They believed that the priests could help decide a person's fate after death.

Immediately after someone died, a chief priest would send a servant to summon other priests. They would be needed to help embalm the body—a process that stops the body from decaying.

Then, the chief priest would gather his tools and set off for his workshop on the west bank of the Nile River.

Meanwhile, other servants collected the body and carried it to the workshop. There they laid it on a special table, ready for the ceremony to begin.

The chief priest put on a jackal-headed mask to represent Anubis, the Egyptian god of mummification. Then, he slowly washed the body while another priest read magic spells out loud. When the body was clean enough, the embalming process began.

Tools
These tools were used in a ritual intended to enable the mummy to eat and drink in the afterlife.

This ancient Egyptian painting shows a body being washed.

After being washed, the body was left to dry.

Jackal Mask
At embalming ceremonies, jackal–headed masks, such as this pottery one, represented Anubis, god of mummification.

The chief priest picked up an embalming knife and carefully made a long cut down the left side of the body. Then he put his hand into the cut and pulled out the liver, lungs, stomach, and guts. Each of these was stored in a canopic jar—a special container in the shape of a god.

The next part was difficult. He had to push a thin bronze hook up the dead person's nose and, bit by bit, scoop out the brain.

Incision
A cut was usually made down the left side of the body.

Embalming knife
This ceremonial knife has a sharp blade made of flint.

Hapy (HAH-pee) was a baboon god who guarded the lungs.

The falcon god Qebehsenuef (keb-ekh-SEN-oo-ef) guarded the intestines, or guts.

The brain was thrown away because the ancient Egyptians did not understand what it was for, so they did not think it was important.

After this, the body was ready to be dried. The priests heaped natron, a natural salt, over the body to draw out all the fluids. It would take 40 days for the body to dry completely.

Only then would the body be ready for the next step.

Natron
This natural salt is found by the edges of desert lakes.

Magical Figures
These figures lay on the body to guard the places where the organs had been removed.

Son of Horus
The four gods who guarded canopic jars were the sons of Horus, god of the sky.

Imsety (im-SET-ee) was a human-like god who guarded the liver.

The jackal-headed god Duamutef (do-ah-MOO-tef) guarded the stomach.

11

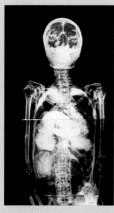

Stuffing
This x-ray of a mummy shows linen stuffing replacing some of the organs.

Scarab beetle

Wadjet eye

Amulets
These were good luck charms. The wadjet eye was believed to keep away evil.

After 40 days, the dried body was filled with linen, sand, or sawdust to help it keep its shape. Beeswax was pushed into the nostrils, and linen was stuffed into the eye sockets. Next, oils and spices were rubbed into the skin to keep it from cracking.

Now the chief priest was ready to begin wrapping the body. He wound thin linen strips around each finger. Then, he bandaged the arms and legs and the rest of the body.

Magical figures called amulets were wrapped in between the layers of cloth. At the same time, the priest brushed the bandages with resin to stick them together. Bandaging the body could take 15 days.

Finally, the mummified body was placed in a coffin. If everything had gone well, the chief priest was pleased. All the dead person needed now was some magic spells.

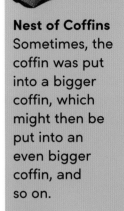

Nest of Coffins
Sometimes, the coffin was put into a bigger coffin, which might then be put into an even bigger coffin, and so on.

Scribes
In ancient Egypt, only scribes could write. They were highly respected people.

Scary Figures
Figures like this hippo were put in the tomb to scare off intruders.

A scribe, or writer, handed the priests a scroll. The scroll was the *Book of the Dead*—a special book containing more than 200 spells. It was placed inside the coffin.

The ancient Egyptians believed that the dead person would need to recite the spells in the book to gain protection on his or her journey to the Hall of the Two Truths.

Hapy, the baboon god

The "Devourer of the Dead" waiting to eat the hearts of evil people

Anubis, god of mummification

Feather of truth

Heart of the dead person

In this judgment hall, the great god Osiris was believed to watch over a ceremony where the dead person had to deny all his or her bad deeds.

Anubis, the jackal-headed god, used scales to balance the person's heart against the "feather of truth." If the heart was not too heavy with bad deeds, the dead person was allowed to live in the afterlife.

Back in this world, the dead person's family filled a tomb with food and treasures for the mummy to use in the afterlife. Curses were often written over the coffin and the walls of the tomb, warning intruders of terrible punishments for stealing.

But over the centuries, grave robbers broke into the tombs looking for treasure. A legend grew that somewhere in the Egyptian Valley of the Kings lay a rich, untouched tomb—the tomb of the young pharaoh Tutankhamun.

Underworld
It was thought that everyone passed through this land on their way to the afterlife. They began their journey by crossing the Nile River.

God of Death
Osiris was king of the afterworld, which was thought to be like Egypt but better.

Howard Carter
After traveling to Egypt as a young artist, Carter's interest turned to investigating ancient Egypt.

Pharaoh
The pharaohs were the kings of ancient Egypt. They were believed to be living gods.

THE MUMMY'S CURSE

"I must find the lost tomb."

Howard Carter had been saying the same thing for years. Now it was 1922, the fifth year he had spent digging through sand and rocks in Egypt's Valley of the Kings. He was searching for a tomb that no grave robbers had ever found—the tomb of Tutankhamun, the boy pharaoh.

Carter scoffed when he was warned of the curse: "Death comes on wings to he who enters the tomb of a pharaoh."

Each day, his team worked in the sweltering heat and dust. They seemed to be getting nowhere. Then, one morning, as they dug in soft rubble, a shovel clanged.

When Carter arrived, he was met by an excited hush. The team had found a stone step. Another 15 steps were quickly uncovered. Could this be Tutankhamun's tomb?

Tutankhamun
This pharaoh ruled from around 1361 BCE to 1352 BCE. He was 19 years old when he died.

Valley of the Kings
To avoid grave robbers, many pharaohs chose this remote place for their tombs.

Carnarvon
This wealthy English lord visited Egypt for his health. His interest in tombs began as a way to pass the time.

Hieroglyphs
Each symbol in this ancient Egyptian writing stands for a word or a sound.

The staircase led to a sealed door. Carter wanted to open it, but he had to wait. Lord Carnarvon, his patron, had paid for the years of work and wanted to be present at the opening.

Today, it would take only six hours to reach Egypt from Carnarvon's home in England, but at that time, it took more than two weeks. When Carnarvon finally arrived, he hurried to the tomb. Nervously, he fingered the strange symbols, called hieroglyphs, by the door. Then, he and Carter opened the door and crept inside.

The two men pushed their way through a rock-filled corridor, which led to another sealed door. Cautiously, they made a hole in the door.

Carter was the first to look. What he saw left him speechless. Later, he told people that he had seen "strange animals, statues, and gold—everywhere the glint of gold."

The room was untidily packed with priceless treasures. There were sparkling gems, animal-shaped beds, beautiful painted boxes, and a magnificent golden throne.

Nothing had been touched for 3,000 years!

Wide-eyed, the pair picked their way through the riches. Then, they came to a third sealed doorway. They were desperate to know where it led, but again they had to wait. First, all these things had to be carefully sorted.

Tomb Jewels
This vulture represented the goddess Nekhabet, and this scarab beetle ornament represented the sun god Khepri.

The paintings on this treasure chest show Tutankhamun conquering his enemies.

Afterlife of Luxury
The ancient Egyptians filled the king's tomb with treasure, such as golden sandals and precious jewels, for him to use in the afterlife.

Kingly Killer
While the cobra can kill people if disturbed, it also helps rid towns of rats and mice.

Royal Dummy
Statues of Tutankhamun often show a cobra on his headdress. This wooden statue is a dummy found in the tomb.

When Carter arrived home that night, his servants were wailing and shouting.

"What's wrong?" Carter demanded above the din.

"You have opened the tomb," wept a servant. "We are cursed!" He told Carter that a cobra had swallowed Carter's pet canary at the exact moment the tomb was opened. Cobras were a symbol of royalty in ancient Egypt. They were said to spit fire at a pharaoh's enemies.

Carter was not worried. The next day, he began to clear the first room of the tomb.

More than a mile of cotton wadding was used to wrap up the items. Carter's team packed games, clothing, pottery, musical instruments, and statues. Most of these were sent to Cairo, Egypt's capital, by boat. The more valuable artifacts went on a train accompanied by armed guards.

Finally, they were ready to unseal the third door. Slowly and carefully, Carter started chipping away the rocks and plaster. Then, he stopped. Before him was a wall of solid gold! It was the front of a huge, golden shrine. Carter was astonished. He knew this was the greatest ancient Egyptian find ever.

Cairo
Egypt's capital city grew up 1,000 years after the death of the last pharaoh.

Howard Carter (left) and his assistants carefully wrap a life-size statue.

Kingly Coffin
The middle coffin was made of wood covered in gold with inlaid glass.

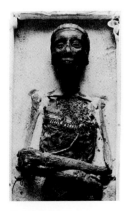

Royal Mummy
Although the riches in the tomb were in good condition, Tutankhamun's mummy was badly decayed.

Inside the golden shrine were three more shrines. And inside the last one was a sarcophagus—a stone coffin. But that was not all. Within the sarcophagus were three more coffins, each fitting snugly inside the other. The final coffin was made of solid gold. Inside it was the mummified body of Tutankhamun.

But before anyone could investigate further, disaster struck. It began when Carter's patron, Lord Carnarvon, was bitten on the cheek by a mosquito.

He accidentally cut open the bite while shaving. The bite soon became infected, and fever set in.

A few days later, Carnarvon's family raced to his bedside. He was very ill. Then, early one morning, it was all over. Lord Carnarvon died.

At the very moment of his death, all the lights in Cairo went out. They stayed out for several hours, and no one could explain why. Back at Lord Carnarvon's home in England, Susie, his dog, pricked up her ears, howled once, then dropped dead.

Other deaths followed. A French scientist who visited the tomb died after a fall. An x-ray specialist on his way to examine Tutankhamun's mummy died unexpectedly. Then, an American died from a virus after visiting the tomb. Were these deaths all coincidences, or was the curse of the mummy to blame? No one knows for sure.

Despite the threat of a curse, many objects have been removed from Egyptian tombs over time. It is now illegal to take these items out of the country. Egyptian authorities have retrieved many items as they work to restore their country's heritage.

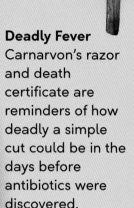

Deadly Fever
Carnarvon's razor and death certificate are reminders of how deadly a simple cut could be in the days before antibiotics were discovered.

A Royal Match
In 1902, Carter found the tomb of Queen Hatshepsut, a famous female pharaoh who ruled Egypt in the 15th century BCE. In 2006, a team of researchers returned to the site. They found a tooth in a box that bore the queen's name. The tooth matched a gap in the jaw of a mummy lying in the tomb.

INCA EMPEROR MUMMIES

As dawn broke, drumbeats sounded through the city of Cuzco (KOOZ-koe). The people began to wake, and an excited buzz filled the air. It was the most important day of the year in the Inca Empire, a civilization that covered much of South America 500 years ago.

Today was Inti Raimi (IN-tee RYE-me), a religious festival held in honor of Inti, the sun god. Every year, this festival was celebrated on June 21, midwinter's day. By showing thanks and honoring Inti, the Inca people believed that summer would come once more and their crops would grow.

Temples were built from carefully shaped blocks of stone. Sun temples were often filled with solid gold models of cornstalks, lumps of earth, and other things related to farming.

Everyone in the Inca Empire gave one-third of all they produced to the priests of the sun god. Many of these plants and animals were sacrificed in special ceremonies held throughout the year. Today's ceremonies were the most important of all.

Inca Year
The Incas had a religious festival for each month. Inti Raimi was held in June, which is the coldest month of the year in South America.

Priests began to chant in time with the drumbeats. In the Holy Square, a large crowd gathered. The people were excited but quiet and respectful. They were waiting for the Procession of the Living Dead.

Sun Disc
The sun god was represented in many Inca temples by gold discs with human faces.

Llamas
The llama is related to the camel. Llamas are still used in South America for wool, meat, and transportation.

At last, the crowds spotted the white llamas that always led the procession. There were hundreds of llamas walking in lines, one after another.

Behind the llamas came a litter carrying the emperor, the Sapa Inca. Everyone in the crowd knelt down, hid their faces in their hands, and prayed. Ordinary people were not allowed to look at the Sapa Inca.

Next came litters, or stretchers, bearing the mummified bodies of the long-dead former Sapa Incas.

Each mummy was worshipped as a son of the sun god. It was thought that the living Sapa Inca received advice and help from these mummies.

Sometimes, a child would sneak a look. He or she would glimpse the mummies, each draped in beautiful cloth woven from the soft wool of the vicuna, a relative of the llama.

But even a peeking child would not see the emperors' faces. They were covered with golden masks, which the priests believed would protect the emperors in the afterlife.

Litters
These beds, or stretchers, were used to carry the mummies in processions.

Huari Mummy
The Huari people lived near Cuzco before the Incas. They too mummified their leaders.

Gods
Incas had great respect for their gods. They gave them offerings, such as statues, gold, animals, and sometimes even people.

Chica
This alcoholic drink was made from corn. It was stored in decorated clay jars.

The procession stopped at the Temple of the Sun, where more ceremonies began. It was a long day, full of prayer. The people thought that if they pleased the mummified Sapa Incas, they would please the sun god.

In the evening, things became a little more festive. The city's inhabitants feasted on roasted llamas served with corn cakes and potatoes. The adults drank freshly brewed chica, an alcoholic drink. There was singing and dancing until late at night. But even during the feast, the sun god was not forgotten. The very best food was put in front of the god's sons, the mummified emperors.

At the end of the day, the mummies were returned to the palaces where they had lived when they were alive. These palaces were still kept in order by specially chosen workers.

The workers fanned the air to keep flies off the mummies. They offered the mummies food and water when they felt it was needed. Most importantly, they delivered messages to the mummies and interpreted their replies.

The people believed that long-gone ancestors could give advice. It did not matter that these emperors were dead—they were still considered very powerful.

Mummified Bodies
For more than 4,000 years, people across South America mummified their dead.

After the Spaniards conquered the Incas in 1532, they built a church on the site of the old Temple of the Sun in Cuzco.

The Andes
This is the longest chain of mountains in the world. The Andes' snowcapped peaks run through Peru and Chile.

Look-Alike
The goddess statue was made of gold and dressed in clothes similar to the girl's.

INCA ICE MAIDEN

The climbers were weary. It had taken three days to reach the top of Nevado Ampato, a high mountain in the Peruvian Andes. The paths were steep and the air was thin, making it difficult to breathe. But finally the four priests reached their destination—the top of the icy ridge.

From packs tied to the llamas, they unloaded pots, food, figurines, and a small statue of a goddess. Then, they set up a small stone altar.

With the group of priests was a 13-year-old girl, the daughter of an important Inca family. Under a warm blanket, she wore a beautiful belted dress of rich yellow, purple, and red wool.

One of the priests led the girl to the altar. She took off the blankets, and the priest draped a finely woven cloth over her shoulders. He fastened the cloth with a silver pin.

Finally, while chanting special prayers, the chief priest placed a large feathered headdress on the girl's head.

Headdress
The girl's headdress was made of macaw feathers. These bird feathers were often used in religious ceremonies.

Last Resort
The Incas stored food in case of a famine. But if there was a long famine, the people appealed to the gods.

Llama Herd
Statues were often used in ceremonies. This llama statue may have reminded the gods to provide grass for their herds to eat.

The unusual group had traveled to the mountain because of a severe three-year drought, or water shortage. Crops had failed, and the people were starving. The priests believed that the drought occurred because the gods were angry.

After much prayer and talk, they had decided that a special sacrifice should be made to the mountain god—they must sacrifice someone who was almost perfect. That person would live forever with the gods in the afterlife. Such a sacrifice would surely please the gods and bring rain.

The girl and her family were a little frightened when she was chosen, but they also felt very honored.

Now the girl sat by a fire as the priests dug a large hole in the frozen ground. They lined the hole with sacred red earth, then placed cups, pots, and food in it for the girl to use in the afterlife.

The priests' chanting grew louder. It was time. The chief priest bent down to hand the girl a strong drink. After a few sips, she slipped into unconsciousness and died. Her body was gently wrapped in thick cloth and laid in the tomb.

When a volcano erupted 500 years later, ash fell on Nevado Ampato, melting the ice. In September 1995, scientists studying the damage found the girl's body. It had been mummified by the freezing cold. Her face had decayed, but the rest of her body was still in almost perfect condition.

Mountain Discovery
The two men who discovered the girl's body carried it down the mountain as fast as they could so it would not thaw and decay. It is now stored in a freezer at a university in Peru, where it is studied and preserved.

SICILIAN MUMMIES

In the Sicilian city of Palermo, an unusual, centuries-old tradition continued right up until the 1920s.

Deep below a Catholic church was an underground cemetery, called a catacomb. It housed the mummified bodies of 6,000 people! Instead of being horrified, locals would often visit the catacomb. In the cool, dark corridors, a child would be unafraid to raise a creaking coffin lid. Inside could be the body of the child's own great-grandmother!

Palermo
This is the largest city on the Italian island of Sicily.

Picnics
Families often made visits to the cemetery and would take a picnic lunch!

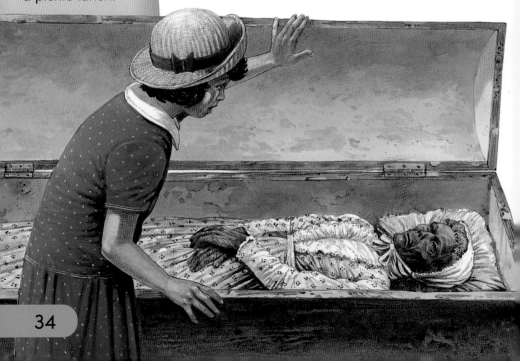

Many of the mummies lie on benches. Labels tell visitors who they are.

Tourist Attraction
Today, the mummies of Sicily attract thousands of visitors from all over the world.

Monk
Palermo's first mummies were the bodies of highly respected monks.

The people went to pay their respects to the mummies, to tell them stories, and to ask their advice. They did not find the mummies upsetting because their families had been visiting the cemetery for more than 300 years. It was simply part of ordinary life. They believed the mummies were a link with loved and respected relatives who had died.

Occasionally, the visitors would see a hooded figure moving silently among the coffins.

Again they were unafraid. They knew it was just one of the monks who looked after the catacomb.

These bearded and robed priests lived in a monastery next to the church. Since 1599, they had been mummifying the bodies of respected monks. Other people soon discovered what was happening and began asking for their relatives' bodies to be mummified in return for a donation to the church. They dressed the dead person in his or her best clothes before taking the body to the monastery.

Monks
The monks who look after the catacomb today still wear the brown robes they have worn for hundreds of years.

Clothing
The mummies provide us with information about the styles of clothes people wore in the past.

Father da Grubbio

This monk died in 1599. The monks today give him a gentle dusting with a vacuum cleaner each year.

The mummification process took over a year to complete—but how it was done was kept secret for hundreds of years!

Some of the mummies are quite gruesome to look at. The mummy of Father Silvestro da Grubbio, the oldest mummy of all, has four laughing skulls displayed around it. When Father da Grubbio died, his body was taken to a special cellar, where it lay over clay pipes for a whole year. This allowed all the body fluids to drain away.

These pipes were used to drain the bodies.

After that, the monks laid the body in the hot Sicilian sun to dry out. Then, they washed it in vinegar and, last of all, wrapped it in straw and sweet-smelling herbs. In spite of this, Father da Grubbio's mummy now looks more like a dressed skeleton.

As time went by, the monks improved their embalming process. Their new methods included soaking the body in arsenic or milk of magnesia. This left the skin far softer and gave it a more lifelike color.

The monks stopped mummifying bodies in 1920, but the mummies are still there. Today, the monks take tourists around the catacomb.

Soft Skin
The mummies made in the 1800s still have their skin and hair today.

Juan Perón
Perón was elected president of Argentina in 1946.

Buenos Aires
Evita was 15 years old when she went to live alone in Argentina's capital city.

THE MUMMY MYSTERY

On July 26, 1952, Pedro Ara's phone rang. "Come quickly," said the caller, "Evita is dying. President Perón is asking for you."

After a year's illness, Evita, the Argentinian president's wife, was dying of cancer.

During her life, Evita had won the hearts of the people. She had set up hospitals and helped the poor. She had also made sure that women in Argentina were allowed to vote.

The president wanted to make sure the people never forgot his wife. He hired Ara, a doctor and expert embalmer, to preserve her body. The president planned to erect a building, called Monument to the People, where Evita would rest.

At 8:25 pm, Evita died. Ara immediately began his secret work. Slowly and carefully, he replaced Evita's blood with glycerol, a thick liquid that would not decay. Then, he placed chemicals in her coffin to kill any insects or bacteria that might attack the body.

Evita's body was then dressed in a white gown and placed in a glass-topped coffin. For 16 days, more than 2,000,000 visitors filed past the coffin on display, many weeping and bending to kiss the glass lid.

But Ara began to worry. The glass case was opened twice to wipe away mist on the inside. It was not good for air to get to the body.

Evita
Evita was born Maria Eva Duarte, the youngest child in a poor family. She later became a popular actress and met many important people, including Juan Perón.

Evita was a passionate speaker loved by many Argentinians.

Sleeping Beauty
Many people who visited Evita's coffin dressed in black or wore their best clothes as a sign of respect.

Resting Place
Evita's body now rests in Recoleta Cemetery in Buenos Aires. It is said to lie in a bombproof compartment.

The coffin was taken to Ara's laboratory. There the body was repeatedly soaked in a bath of chemicals and injected with more preservatives. Finally, it was covered in a thin layer of clear plastic. It took Ara a year to complete the work, but he knew that the body would last forever.

Meanwhile, life in Argentina had become unsettled. President Perón had been overthrown by the army and forced to leave the country.

The new ruler, President Pedro Aramburu, did not want anything around that might encourage Perón's supporters. He canceled the plans for the Monument to the People and looked for somewhere else to place Evita's body.

Colonel Carlos Koenig, head of Army Intelligence, offered help. Shortly afterward, in November 1955, the body disappeared. Many stories began to circulate around Argentina about where it had gone.

After Aramburu's death in 1970, his lawyer handed over an envelope that solved the mystery.

In September 1971, gravediggers at an Italian cemetery were told to open the tomb of a woman called Maria Maggi de Magistris.

Inside the tomb was a perfectly preserved body. But it was not Maria Maggi. It was Evita Perón! The body had been secretly buried there 14 years earlier.

In 1974, Evita's body was returned to Argentina. She was laid to rest in her family tomb.

A Grieving Nation
People had to wait hours to see Evita's body. The huge crowds stretched for 3 miles (5 km).

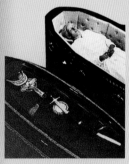

Together Again
In 1974, when Juan Perón died, he was not embalmed. His closed coffin was displayed next to Evita's open one.

Evita at rest in her coffin

MUMMIES TODAY

Protecting the Past
Today, most scientists treat the ancient dead respectfully and make the information they find widely available.

Today's fascination with mummies began when the French general Napoleon Bonaparte invaded Egypt in 1798. Teams of French scholars began to study the ancient Egyptian civilization.

But much of the evidence had already been destroyed. Thousands of mummies had been burned as fuel, ground up for medicine, or simply left to decay.

The first mummies transported to the West were treated little better. Many were "unwrapped" during exhibitions, destroying vital information in the process.

Scientists use mummies to find out what diseases people suffered from in the past. They use microscopes to look at skin, bone, and other body tissues.

Advances in technology have allowed people to take better care of ancient finds. In 1895, x-rays were discovered. An x-ray picture shows scientists what is inside a mummy case. Mummies no longer need to be unwrapped to be studied.

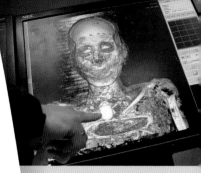

An Inside Look
This x-ray of an Inca mummy shows that the brain has shrunk to a small round ball at the base of the skull.

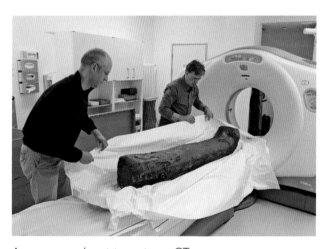

A mummy about to enter a CT scanner

A Peek Inside
A CT scan can show the skin on a mummy's face. At another setting, the machine could show the bone below the skin.

Today, scientists use electronic scanners, called CT scanners, to produce three-dimensional images of a mummy inside its bandages.

GLOSSARY

Afterlife
A life experienced after death.
Different cultures have different
beliefs about the afterlife.

Altar
A table, rock, or platform used in
religious services

Artifact
A human-made object found at the
sites of ancient homes or graves

Bacteria
Small, one-celled organisms. Some
species cause disease or break down
dead matter.

Curse
A wish or spell intended to cause
harm to another person

Embalm
To use chemicals, perfumes, or
ointments to preserve a body

Hieroglyph
(HIE-row-gliff)
A picture or symbol used to stand
for a word or sound in ancient
Egyptian writing

Monk
A man living and working
in a religious community

Mummify
The process of making a body into
a mummy

Mummy
A body that has been preserved
by nature or by people

Natron
A naturally forming salt used by the
ancient Egyptians to absorb fluids

Pharaoh
(FAIR-oh)
The title given to the kings of
ancient Egypt who reigned from
around 3000 BCE to 30 BCE.

Sacrifice
To kill a person or animal in a
ceremony because of a belief that
it will please a god

Shrine
A cabinet for holding a person's
remains; also a place where people
honor the memory of a dead person

Tomb
A grave, monument, or small
building where a dead body
is stored

Tutankhamun
(toot-an-kah-mun)
A boy pharaoh who ruled Egypt
from about 1361 BCE to 1352 BCE

Underworld
The ancient Egyptians believed that
everyone had to travel through this
world beneath the earth on their
journey to the afterlife.

X-rays
Special rays that are used to produce
an image of a person's bones and
internal organs

INDEX

QUIZ

Answer the questions to see what you have learned. Check your answers in the key below.

1. What animals did ancient Egyptians believe were sacred?

2. True or False: Canopic jars were in the shape of different Egyptian gods.

3. What were wrapped in between the layers of a mummy's cloth?

4. The ancient Egyptian god Osiris was king of what?

5. What was Tutankhamun's final coffin made of?

6. What caused the Inca "ice maiden" to mummify?

7. On what Italian island were mummies kept in a catacomb?

8. What do scientists use mummies for?

1. Cats 2. True 3. Amulets 4. The afterworld 5. Solid gold
6. The freezing cold 7. Sicily 8. To find out what diseases people suffered from in the past